100 FASCINATING
BIBLE FACTS

Dedicated to my young friends
to whom I've taught the precious Word of God
in Sunday School:
Eoghan, Neil, Allan, Craig and Joseph,
Callum, Fiona Jean, Heidi, James and Graham,
Stephen, Mark, Richard, Martin and Jonathan,
Leanne, Rhian and Joel,
Sarah, Christopher, Katie and Joanna.

100 FASCINATING
BIBLE FACTS

Irene Howat

CHRISTIAN FOCUS

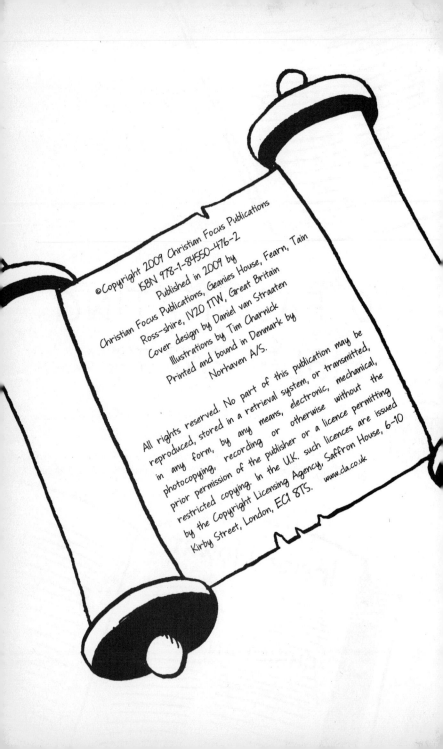

Contents

Join the fact finders to see what you can find out about God's Word the Bible!

Chloe

Chloe is in charge of the quizzes. Let's see how many you get right!

Zach

Zach has some challenges for you to try out. How well do you think you will do?

Abbi

Whenever there is some extra information needed – Abbi is the one with everything to hand!

WHAT IS A FACT?

A fact is something that is certain, sure and true, something so reliable that we can use it as the basis of our lives. The Bible is true because it is the Word of God and God cannot tell lies. Therefore all the stories quoted in this book are factual and true.

1

THE BIBLE
WHAT IS IT?

1

The Bible has a very long history, going right back to the days when people wrote on parchment, and the Egyptian word for parchment was *byblos*. The Greeks used that old Egyptian word to mean a scroll, and they changed it to *biblion*. Their word for a collection of books, a library, was *biblia*. That's where we get the word Bible. Think about it. You know some ancient Egyptian and Greek!

2

Our Bible is divided into two main parts, the Old Testament and the New Testament. What is a testament? You've already discovered a word in Egyptian and another one in Greek. Now for some Latin and Hebrew! *Berith* is the Hebrew word for a pact, or an agreement, or a covenant. The Latin word for a pact is *testamentum* and it's from there that we get the word testament in English. The Old Testament is named after the pact, or covenant, that God made through Abraham with the people of Israel. And the New Testament is named after the pact, or covenant, that God makes through Jesus Christ with all who trust in him.

3

The first book of the Bible is called Genesis. What does that word mean? Well it means 'how something comes into being.' In the Book of Genesis we read about how God brought the world into being or how God created all things. If you want to add to your knowledge of ancient languages, the word 'genesis' had its origins or beginnings in ancient Greek.

ZACH'S CHALLENGE

See if you can draw up a list of all the books in the Bible and then memorise them! Now that's a challenge!

4

The Book of Genesis tells the story of Abram. This name means 'exalted father.' Isn't that a strange name to call your baby son! Presumably his parents hoped that one day he would be a father and that his family would think highly of him. God changed Abram's name to Abraham (Genesis 17:5), which means 'Father of many.' That was an especially good name as the Lord had just told him that he would become the father of many nations!

braham and his wife, Sarah, were much too old to have children. Abraham was nearly 100 years old. But God promised Abraham that he would have a son in a year's time. Sarah overheard what was said and laughed. However, God's promise came true; one year later their little son was born. They called him 'He Laughs'! That's Isaac in Hebrew. (Genesis 21:3-6)

14

ABBI'S PAGE

When God makes a promise it's as good as kept because he keeps all his promises. So the promises God makes in his Word are facts of life for those who trust in him. Here are two fascinating facts that are absolutely certain for every Christian because the Lord in whom they trust does not tell lies.

'If any of you lacks wisdom, he should ask God, who gives generously to all without finding fault, and it will be given to him' (James 1:5).

'Let the wicked forsake his way and the evil man his thoughts. Let him turn to the Lord, and he will have mercy on him, and to our God, for he will freely pardon' (Isaiah 55:7).

Names are given for different reasons. Some people are named after a relative or because their parents liked the name. Abraham's son, Isaac, and his wife, Rebekah, chose unusual names for their twin boys. The first they called Esau, which means red or hairy, for when the baby was born he was both red and hairy. But the other twin was called Jacob, which means 'The Deceiver'. Imagine going through life called The Deceiver! The name suited Jacob because he was a deceiver until the Lord changed his heart. (Genesis 25:25-26)

7

Esau and Jacob got on each other's nerves. They often fought. Eventually Jacob ran away from home to escape his brother, but he could not run away from God. Once he had a dream in which he saw a ladder going from earth to heaven, with angels climbing up and down it. From the top of the ladder God spoke to Jacob, telling him that he and his descendants would be blessed. Jacob named the place where he had his dream Bethel, which means 'House of God' (Genesis 28:19).

Some years later Jacob had a strange experience. He and his family were going to visit Esau. While they were travelling Jacob spent a night wrestling with God. Afterwards God changed Jacob's name to Israel, which means 'He struggles with God' (Genesis 32:28). Israel changed the name of the place to Peniel, which means 'face of God,' because it was there that he had seen the face of God and lived (Genesis 32:30). Jacob's family became known as the Israelites. They were God's chosen people but they didn't have a land of their own. Find out how God gave them their own land in the Book of Exodus.

9

The second book of the Bible is called Exodus. This word means 'a mass departure of people.' What people are we talking about and where were they going? Well at the beginning of the Book of Exodus the Israelites had been slaves in Egypt for a long time. God arranged it so that a man named Moses would lead them out of captivity. Pharaoh, the ruler of Egypt, would not let them go, even though the Lord sent nine plagues on the country. Only after the tenth and most awful plague did Pharaoh allow the Israelites to leave Egypt. About 600,000 men, as well as women and children, departed from Egypt that day. It certainly was a mass departure!

Exodus

10

The Book of Exodus begins with the birth of Moses. As a baby he was hidden in a basket by the river Nile because Pharaoh was attempting to kill all the baby boys that were born to Israelite families. Many people assume that it was his parents, Amram and Jochabed, who came up with the name Moses but it was not. The name Moses means 'draw out' and it was Pharaoh's daughter who gave the boy his name when she discovered him by the river. We don't know what his parents called him (Exodus 2:10).

CHLOE'S QUIZ

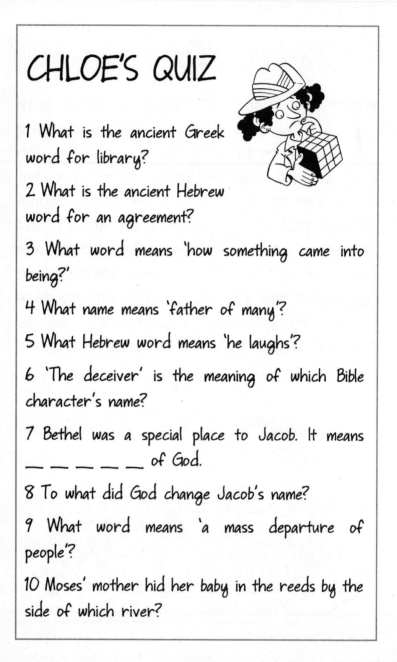

1 What is the ancient Greek word for library?

2 What is the ancient Hebrew word for an agreement?

3 What word means 'how something came into being?'

4 What name means 'father of many'?

5 What Hebrew word means 'he laughs'?

6 'The deceiver' is the meaning of which Bible character's name?

7 Bethel was a special place to Jacob. It means _ _ _ _ _ of God.

8 To what did God change Jacob's name?

9 What word means 'a mass departure of people'?

10 Moses' mother hid her baby in the reeds by the side of which river?

ZACH'S CHALLENGE

Draw a grid twelve squares wide and twelve squares deep. Fit the answers into the grid to create a wordsearch. The words can be written in the ordinary way or backwards or diagonally forwards or backwards. Fill in the empty spaces with letters of your choice. Ask a friend to find your list of answers in the wordsearch.

ABBI'S PAGE

If you want to find out more about Moses' early life, read the Book of Exodus. His sister, Miriam, was watching over him while he was floating in the basket. When Pharaoh's daughter discovered him God gave Miriam a bright idea. She asked the princess if she needed someone to look after the baby. The princess offered to pay a wage to whoever would do it. Miriam fetched her mother, which meant that Amram and Jochabed could bring up their little boy at home in safety!

It is amazing to see how God's plans always work out. We should ask him to guide us throughout our lives. 'Whether you turn to the right or to the left, your ears will hear a voice behind you, saying, "This is the way; walk in it"' (Isaiah 30:21).

11

When Moses was older he went to live in Pharaoh's palace, but this didn't last. Moses made some bad mistakes and had to run for his life. He became a shepherd in the wilderness and married a woman named Zipporah. One day, when he was in the desert with his sheep, Moses saw a bush burning that was not burnt out. From the burning bush the Lord spoke to him. God told Moses that he had been chosen to save the children of Israel from the Egyptians. Moses asked God what his name was in order that he could tell the people who had sent him. God told Moses his name. His name is 'I am who I am.' Moses had to tell the Israelites that 'I AM' had sent him (Exodus 3:14).

Eventually Pharaoh released the Israelites from slavery, but only after God had sent terrible plagues on the land. One of the plagues was an infestation of frogs! They got everywhere. You can read the list of plagues on page 28. But where would the Israelites go when they left Egypt? God was going to lead

them to a land of their very own called Canaan. Before they got there, however, they wandered in the desert for forty years. During that time they often grumbled about their food. God sent them special food called manna that lay like frost on the ground. Manna means 'What is it?' and you can just imagine the first time they saw it. They would all look puzzled and ask each other, 'What is it?' And the name stuck! (Exodus 16:31)

When the Children of Israel went into God's Promised Land, all the tribes were given land except for the tribe of Levi. The Levites were chosen by God to arrange his worship and the other tribes had to provide for them from the fruit of the land they had been given. The Book of Leviticus describes the work that the Lord wanted the Levites to do. So it contains instructions for the offerings God wanted made to him along with details of how the Levites had to care for the people. God was interested in every part of their lives, and the Levites learned about offerings, skin complaints, mildew in houses, food regulations, crime and punishment and many other things as well. The book name Leviticus comes from the word Levi.

Leviticus

ABBI'S PAGE

HERE ARE THE TEN
COMMANDMENTS:

1. You shall have no other gods before me.
2. You shall not worship idols.
3. Do not misuse the name of the Lord your God.
4. Keep the Lord's day holy. Six days you shall work but the seventh day is a day of rest.
5. Honour your father and your mother so that your days may be long in the land that God has given you.
6. Do not murder.
7. Do not commit adultery.
8. Do not steal.
9. Do not lie.
10. Do not covet what belongs to other people.

ABBI'S PAGE

HERE IS A LIST OF THE TEN PLAGUES:

1. The River Nile was turned to blood.
2. Hordes of frogs.
3. Gnat infestation.
4. Swarms of Flies.
5. The Livestock dies.
6. All Egyptians afflicted by boils and sores.
7. A horrific hail storm destroyed the crops.
8. A swarm of locusts ate all vegetation in sight.
9. Complete darkness for three whole days.
10. The first-born in every Egyptian family died.

The Israelites did not suffer from the plagues as they lived apart from the Egyptian people in Goshen. When the final and terrible plague of death arrived the Israelites were instructed to paint their doorposts and lintles with the blood of a lamb. When the Angel of Death saw the blood they would be safe.

14

The name of the fourth book of the Bible is Numbers because it's full of ... numbers! Moses was told by the Lord to take a census of the whole Israelite community. He did that, and what a job it must have been. At the time of the census the descendants of Jacob, aged twenty and over, and able to serve in the army, came to an amazing 603,550 (Numbers 1:46).

Deuteronomy

15

The fifth book of the Bible is Deuteronomy. This comes from two Greek words *deuteros*, meaning second, and *nomos*, meaning law. It is the second book of the Bible containing the Ten Commandments, therefore it's the second book of the Law. The Ten Commandments are in Exodus 20 and Deuteronomy 5. Deuteronomy also contains many other laws given by God.

Joshua

Joshua is the sixth book of the Bible and is called after the Israelite leader, Joshua, who succeeded Moses. When Joshua died there was nobody to take over from him. Instead of having one leader, God gave his people a series of fifteen judges, whose job was to keep the Israelites living how the Lord wanted them to live. The people failed God often, but he never once failed them. The story of the fifteen judges is told in the book named ... Judges. It's obvious, isn't it?

17

Many of the books of the Bible are named after the people who wrote them, or the people about whom the books are written. The Book of Ruth is a love story with a twist, because at the end of the story Ruth and her husband, Boaz, have a little baby boy who turns out to be the grandfather of King David and the great, great, (27 greats!) grandfather of the Lord Jesus Christ! The two books of Samuel tell the story of that great man of God, David, who led God's people through a really difficult time of their history.

Ruth

The children of Israel had a King; God was their King. That didn't satisfy them and they wanted to be like all the countries round about them who had human kings at the head of their armies. Four books of the Bible tell the story of that part of history: 1 & 2 Kings and 1 & 2 Chronicles. The word 'chronicles' means 'a detailed record of events.' So these books are detailed records of the history of the kings of Israel.

Ezra

19

Because they had disobeyed God so often and so seriously, the Lord exiled the children of Israel to Babylon and allowed Jerusalem to be destroyed, temple and all. Ezra lived when Jerusalem and its temple were being rebuilt towards the end of the exile. He was able to tell the people what God's Law said. The book of Ezra is named after him. His story is also told in Nehemiah.

20

The book of Nehemiah is named after ... Nehemiah. No surprises there! Nehemiah worked in the King of Babylon's palace but he was given time off to organize the rebuilding of the walls of Jerusalem. Three wicked men tried to put him off the work, inviting him to a place called Ono to discuss things. Nehemiah knew better. When asked to go to Ono, he said, 'Oh no!' or words to that effect!

The Book of Esther is named after an Israelite woman who became Queen of Babylon. She was used by the Lord to save her people from extermination. Interestingly, the words 'God' and 'Lord' don't appear in the Book of Esther at all even though she was a woman of great faith and courage.

22

The next five books of the Bible are known as the Books of Wisdom: Job, Psalms, Proverbs, Ecclesiastes and Song of Solomon. Here are two pieces of wise advice taken from them. 'Remember your Creator in the days of your youth ...' (Ecclesiastes 12:1), and 'Like a gold ring in a pig's snout is a beautiful woman who shows no discretion' (Proverbs 11:22).

From there to the end of the Old Testament (with one exception), the books are named after God's prophets – godly men who told the people what the Lord wanted them to know. These books are: Isaiah, Jeremiah, Ezekiel, Daniel, Hosea, Joel, Amos, Obadiah, Jonah, Micah, Nahum, Habakkuk, Zephaniah, Haggai, Zechariah and Malachi.

The Prophets

CHLOE'S QUIZ

On a separate sheet
of paper answer
these quiz questions.

11 Write down the
five words that are
names of God.

12 With what special food did God feed his
people in the wilderness?

13 What group of people are linked to the third
book of the Bible?

14 What is the fourth book of the Bible full of?

15 What Greek word means second?

16 The sixth book of the Bible was called after
which great leader?

17 Two books in the Old Testament tell the story
of another great man of God. Who was he?

18 What word means 'a detailed record of events'?

19 To which country did God exile his disobedient people?

20 Nehemiah organised the rebuilding of the walls of which city?

21 Esther was a woman of great faith and

_ _ _ _ _ _ _.

22 The books of Job, Psalms, Proverbs, Ecclesiastes and Song of Solomon are together known as the Books of what?

23 Most of the Old Testament books are named after God's what?

The exception is the Book of Lamentations written by Jeremiah. It was given its name because he was lamenting, or mourning, the destruction of the first temple in Jerusalem. Yet in the middle of the book he says some encouraging words. 'Because of the Lord's great love we are not consumed, for his compassions never fail. They are new every morning; great is your faithfulness' (Lamentations 3:22-23). This reminds us that even when life is difficult God cares for his people.

Lamentations

The names of the first four books of the New Testament are the names of the four men who wrote them. Matthew, the tax collector, followed Jesus and became his disciple (Matthew 9:9). Mark, whose first name was John, was the son of Mary, in whose home it's thought that the Last Supper was held (Acts 12:12). Luke was a doctor who joined Paul in his missionary work (Colossians 4:14). John and his brother James were among Jesus' first followers (Mark 1:19-20). These four books are called The Gospels.

The Gospels and The Acts of the Apostles

The Book of Acts is a shortened version of the book's name. It's actually called The Acts of the Apostles, and it tells the story of the early church. It was written by Dr Luke and is part two of his gospel story.

The following nine books of the New Testament (they were written as letters) get their names from the people to whom Paul wrote them. Romans, 1 & 2 Corinthians, Galatians, Ephesians, Philippians, Colossians and 1 & 2 Thessalonians were written to groups of Christians in the obvious places - Rome, Galatia, Ephesus, Philippi, Colossae and Thessalonica. Sometimes these books are also known as The Epistles. They were all written by the Apostle Paul.

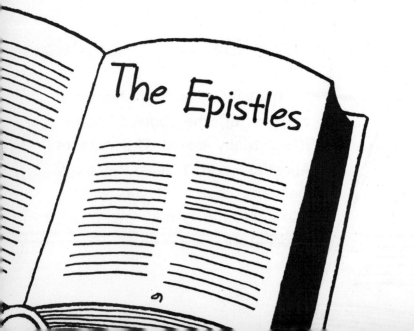

Timothy, Titus and Philemon are the names of individual people to whom Paul wrote letters, and the books of the Bible have been called after them.

45

The Book of Hebrews was written to the children of Israel who believed in the Lord Jesus Christ. They were often called Hebrews, hence the name of the book. Because they knew the Old Testament, much of what the writer to the Hebrews wrote is based on how Jesus fits into Old Testament teaching.

The next seven books are called after the people who wrote them: James, Peter, John and Jude. Peter and John were Jesus' disciples. Peter was the one who denied Jesus three times. James and Jude were two of Jesus' brothers.

The final book of the New Testament, and of the whole Bible, is named Revelation, or the Revelation of John. A revelation is something that's made known, and in this wonderful book God made known to John in a vision some amazing facts about heaven. Here is one of them. 'I saw the Holy City, the new Jerusalem, coming down out of heaven from

God, prepared as a bride beautifully dressed for her husband ...' (Revelation 21:2). And a little further on, John saw that '... God himself will be with them and be their God. He will wipe every tear from their eyes. There will be no more death or mourning or crying or pain ...' (verses 3-4). Much of John's vision is too amazing for our human minds to take in, but from it we know that heaven will be wonderful beyond anything we can think or imagine.

2

JESUS —
HIS BIRTH

Throughout Old Testament times God told his people about the Saviour who was to come. He didn't tell them everything, but little by little over many years a picture built up. Then, when the Lord Jesus Christ was born, those who knew their Bibles could see things falling into place. Here are some fascinating facts that show prophecies being fulfilled 700 — 800 years after they were made!

Prophecy: 'But you, Bethlehem Ephrathah, though you are small among the clans of Judah, out of you will come for me one who will be ruler over Israel, whose origins are from of old, from ancient times' (Micah 5:2).

Fulfilment: An angel from the Lord told some shepherds that the Saviour had been born. When the angels left them, the shepherds said to one another, "Let's go to Bethlehem and see this thing that has happened, which the Lord has told us about." So they hurried off and found Mary and Joseph, and the baby, who was lying in the manger (Luke 2:15-16).

Micah 5:2
Luke 2:15-16

ZACH'S CHALLENGE

Can you match a Bible story to every place on the map? Now that's quite a challenge!

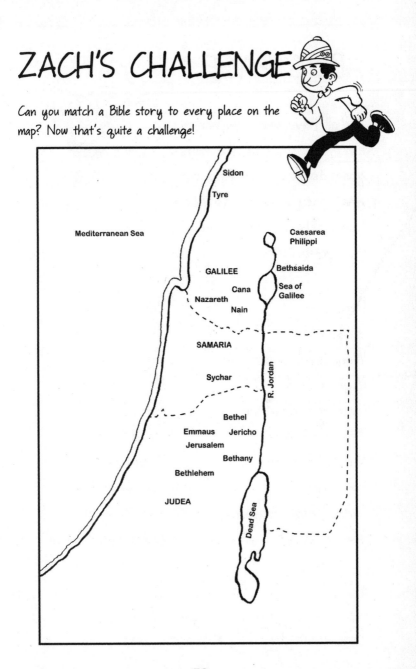

ABBI'S PAGE

We all have our own names.
Here are some of the names
given to Jesus. To find out
what they mean go to Abbi's
Extra Bits at the end of the book.

Redeemer

Immanuel

Wonderful Counsellor

Mighty God

Everlasting Father

Prince of Peace

Man of Sorrows

Fountain

Sun of Righteousness

Son of God

Jesus – Saviour

The Word

The Lamb

Messiah/Christ

Son of David

Good Shepherd

Bread of Life

The True Vine

The Mediator

Alpha and Omega

Prophecy: 'Therefore the Lord himself will give you a sign: The virgin will be with child and will give birth to a son, and will call him Immanuel' (Isaiah 7:14).

Fulfilment: 'In the sixth month, God sent the angel Gabriel to Nazareth, a town in Galilee, to a virgin ...' The angel said to her, 'Do not be afraid, Mary, you have found favour with God. You will be with child and give birth to a son, and you are to give him the name Jesus.' (Luke 1:26, 30-31) Immanuel means 'God with us' and, when Jesus was born, God was with the human race in a very special way.

Isaiah 7:14
Luke 1:26,
30-31

34

Prophecy: 'The kings of Tarshish and of distant shores will bring tribute to him; the kings of Sheba and Seba will present him gifts' (Psalm 72:10).

Fulfilment: 'After Jesus was born in Bethlehem in Judea, during the time of King Herod, Magi from the east came to Jerusalem and asked, "Where is the one who has been born king of the Jews? We saw his star in the east and have come to worship him ..." On coming to the house, they saw the child with his mother Mary, and... worshipped him. Then they opened their treasures and presented him with gold, incense and myrrh' (Matthew 2:1-2, 11).

Psalm 72:10
Matthew
2:1-2, 11

Prophecy: 'When Israel was a child, I loved him, and out of Egypt I called my son' (Hosea 11:1).

Fulfilment: 'When they (the Magi) had gone, an angel of the Lord appeared to Joseph in a dream. "Get up," he said, "take the child and his mother and escape to Egypt. Stay there until I tell you, for Herod is going to search for the child to kill him." So he got up, took the child and his mother during the night and left for Egypt. … After Herod died, an angel of the Lord appeared in a dream to Joseph in Egypt and said, "Get up, take the child and his mother and go to the land of Israel, for those who were trying to take the child's life are dead"' (Matthew 2:13-15, 19-20).

Matthew 2:13-15, 19-20

Hosea 11:1

CHLOE'S QUIZ

On a separate sheet of paper answer these questions. Be careful because Zach has a challenge for you afterwards!

24 Who wrote the Book of Lamentations?

25 Which doctor joined Paul in his missionary work?

26 The Book of Acts tells of the acts of the
_ _ _ _ _ _ _ _.

27 Who wrote many books of the New Testament, including the letter to Christians at Rome?

28 Paul wrote letters to Timothy, Titus and who else?

29 Which New Testament book was written to the children of Israel who believed in Jesus?

30 Who else was a brother of James and Jude?

31 The Revelation of St John is a wonderful vision of what?

32 To what town did the shepherds go to see the newborn Jesus?

33 What word means 'God with us'?

34 The Magi brought gifts to the boy Jesus. The gifts were gold, incense and what else?

35 To what land did God tell Joseph to take Mary and their son Jesus?

ZACH'S CHALLENGE

If you have answered the questions correctly, only six letters of the alphabet will not appear in your answers. What are they? Turn the book upside down for the answer.

(THE ANSWER IS C, D, F, Q, X AND Z)

Prophecy: 'This is what the Lord says: "A voice is heard in Ramah, mourning and great weeping, Rachel weeping for her children and refusing to be comforted, because her children are no more"' (Jeremiah 31:15).

Fulfilment: 'When Herod realised that he had been outwitted by the Magi, he was furious, and he gave orders to kill all the boys in Bethlehem and its vicinity who were two years old and under, in accordance with the time he had learned from the Magi' (Matthew 2:16). No wonder the poor women were weeping.

Jeremiah 31:15
Matthew 2:16

JESUS - HIS MIRACLES

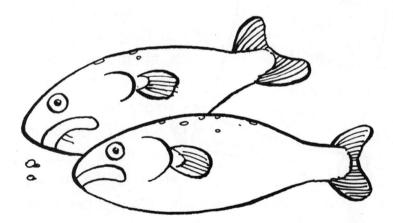

37

What's a miracle? A miracle is something quite outside of what happens naturally. It is truly supernatural. There are miracles in the Bible apart from those done by Jesus, but we'll stick to the ones he did. We should not be surprised that Jesus did miracles. Why should the one who made the laws of nature not change or suspend them if he chooses to? Perhaps the biggest miracle of all, and it truly is a miracle, is that the Lord Jesus Christ, the king of Kings and lord of Lords, should come down from his throne of glory and humble himself, becoming a little baby in order to die to save us from our sins. We just can't take that in! (Philippians 2:6-8)

Jesus' Humility and Power to Save

*O*ne day a man suffering from leprosy came to Jesus and knelt before him. 'Lord, if you are willing, you can make me clean.' That poor man was absolutely right in what he said. Jesus is able to do anything he is willing to do. Before he healed the man, Jesus reached out and touched him. Lepers were 'untouchables' but Jesus touched him! The Lord's touch must have been like a bolt of lightning through the man. Then Jesus said, 'I am willing. Be clean.' And he was! (Matthew 8:1-4)

Jesus has power over disease

63

Imagine being invited out for a meal and then arriving to find your hostess in bed with a high temperature. I guess most of us would just go home. Jesus didn't. He healed his hostess who then got up and served the meal! (Matthew 8:14-15)

That same evening many people came to Jesus and were healed of their illnesses and had demons driven out of them by the power of his word. Jesus was not a doctor who gave people medicine that made them better, he was God who commanded diseases and evil spirits to come out of the people they were troubling. (Matthew 8:16)

41

Sometimes what Jesus said sounds really puzzling. Some men brought their paralysed friend to him for help. They probably expected the Lord to tell him to get up and walk. Instead he told the man that his sins were forgiven. No wonder the teachers of the law were furious for only God could do that! But Jesus had chosen his words carefully because he was telling them that he was indeed God. Then he told the man to get up, roll up his mat and go home. How grateful that man must have been – forgiven and healed at the same time! (Matthew 9:1-8)

Jesus has power over evil spirits and sin

Jesus was on his way to heal a dying twelve-year-old girl, when a woman who had been ill for twelve years asked him for healing. While Jesus talked to the woman the little girl died. But Jesus brought her back to life. Then he told her parents to give her something to eat! Life was normal again thanks to Jesus. (Mark 5:21-43)

Some people are never happy. One day a man was brought to Jesus who was possessed by a demon. The demon prevented the man from speaking. Jesus drove the demon out and the man spoke again. The people were amazed, but the teachers of the law decided that the demon obeyed Jesus because Jesus was a demon! How foolish! (Matthew 9:32-34)

44

There was a man who spent his life in a graveyard. He was demon possessed. He had such strength he could break chains and he hurt himself in all sorts of ways. He cried out in his despair night and day. When Jesus arrived this poor man ran and fell on the ground in front of him. He yelled at the Lord not to torture him. As he did so he called Jesus by name for, while men and women don't always recognise who Jesus is, devils do although they don't worship him. This miracle has a very strange ending. The demons were ordered to go into a nearby herd of pigs which then raced down a hill into the sea and drowned. The local people were scared of Jesus and asked him to go away! (Mark 5:1-20)

Jesus has power over death and demons

45

Not all of Jesus' miracles involved making sick people better. Once a huge crowd followed him to hear his teaching. Over 5,000 men, as well as women and children, were there and they were hungry. Jesus asked his disciples how much food there was. All they could find was the magnificent total of five bread rolls and two little fish. What could Jesus do with that? He fed more than 5,000 people that's what! Not only that, but there were piles of leftovers. Jesus never does anything by half! (Mark 6:30-44)

Jesus has power over all creation

Once the Lord performed two miracles on the same man at one time. The man was deaf and unable to speak. He had probably been deaf all of his life and so had never been able to learn how to speak. Not only did Jesus give him the gift of hearing he also gave him the gift of speech. The man was able to say words he had never heard! That would be like you going to the remotest part of Papua New Guinea and being able to speak to people there, never having heard their language before! And it was also a very kind miracle for it saved people laughing at a grown-up trying to learn words for the first time. (Mark 7:31-37)

Jesus has power over our bodies

It wasn't unusual to see blind men begging in Jesus' day. Bartimaeus was doing that in Jericho. He had heard about Jesus and shouted out to the Lord. People told him to be quiet, but he wouldn't stop shouting. Jesus heard and sent for him. 'What do you want me to do for you?' Jesus asked Bartimaeus. 'I want to see,' was his immediate reply. Jesus knew that the blind man believed in him and he healed him. Imagine this – the first person Bartimaeus saw was the Lord Jesus! How lovely! (Mark 10:46-52)

Jesus has power over our abilities

CHLOE'S QUIZ

On a separate sheet of paper answer these quiz questions and then find the odd ones out.

36 Who wept for her children?

37 What is something quite outside of what happens naturally?

38 What was the man suffering from who asked Jesus to make him clean?

39 What did Jesus do to his hostess who was ill?

40 What did Jesus drive out of some poor people?

41 How did the teachers of the law feel when Jesus forgave a man's sins?

42 How old (in a word rather than a number) was the dead girl to whom Jesus gave back her life?

43 How did the crowd react to Jesus making a silent man speak?

44 Where did the demon-possessed man live?

45 What were there piles of after Jesus fed more than 5,000 people?

46 When Jesus healed one man, he gave him two gifts. What were they?

47 What was Bartimaeus before the Lord healed him?

ZACH'S CHALLENGE

Now find the two odd answers out. Only two don't have an E in them. Turn the book upside down for the answers.

(THE ANSWERS ARE FURIOUS AND BLIND)

Jesus was compassionate. When he saw a widow weeping on her way to bury her only son, he told her not to cry. He then told the young man to get up. Life was given back to the woman's son and he sat up and began to talk. Imagine the reaction of the crowd! No wonder news of what happened spread right through the country. (Luke 7:11-17)

Jesus has power over death

Jesus was in the synagogue on the Sabbath day. A woman was there who had been bent over for eighteen years. She wasn't able to straighten up at all. Jesus put his hands on her and told her that she was set free from her problem. Immediately she straightened up and praised God. But guess what! Some people were unhappy that Jesus had healed on the Sabbath, even though they would have looked after their farm animals on the Sabbath. (Luke 13:10-17)

Jesus has power over life

The Lord Jesus Christ didn't even need to be near people to heal them. He could heal them at a distance. Once a royal official came to the Lord and asked him to come to his home to heal his dying son. Jesus told the man to go home and that his son would live. Believing what he was told, the official headed for home. The following day, on his way home, some of his servants came to meet him with the news that his son had recovered. And when the official asked for details, he discovered that the boy became better just at the time Jesus said he would. That's amazing! (John 4:43-53)

Jesus can heal anywhere

One day Jesus healed a man who was born blind. The man's parents were delighted. But the teachers of the law set up a criminal investigation! The man who had been given the gift of sight became exasperated with them and said, 'If *Jesus* were not from God, he could do nothing.' The teachers of the law snapped back, 'You were steeped in sin at birth; how dare you lecture us!' Then they threw the man out of the building. Their reaction is almost as amazing as the miracle itself! (John 9:1-41)

Jesus has power over our abilities

Jesus had three friends in Bethany, Lazarus and his sisters, Mary and Martha. One day Lazarus fell very sick. By the time the Lord and his disciples reached Bethany Lazarus was dead and buried. Jesus stood by the tomb and wept. To everyone's surprise Jesus told the people to take away the stone from the tomb. When that was done, the Lord shouted in a loud voice, telling Lazarus to come out. But dead men can't walk. How amazed people must have been when Lazarus obeyed the voice of Jesus and walked out of the tomb, still bound up in his grave clothes. Even death does what Jesus tells it to do. (John 11:1-44)

Jesus has power over death

THE DEATH OF JESUS
THE FACTS

Like the birth of the Lord Jesus, his death was prophesied throughout the Old Testament. The Lord's coming was not an emergency measure when sin got out of control, his coming was part of the plan of salvation laid before the beginning of time. Here are some of the prophecies that were fulfilled at that sad time.

Jesus was betrayed by one of his friends, one with whom he had just shared the first Communion bread and wine (John 13:18). 'Even my close friend, whom I trusted, he who shared my bread, has lifted up his heel against me' (Psalm 41:9).

Judas betrayed Jesus for thirty pieces of silver (Matthew 26:14-15). 'I told them, "If you think it best, give me my pay; but if not, keep it." So they paid me thirty pieces of silver' (Zechariah 11:12).

Judas' money went to the potter (Matthew 27:7). 'And the Lord said to me, "Throw it to the potter" – the handsome price at which they priced me! So I took the thirty pieces of silver and threw them into the house of the Lord to the potter' (Zechariah 11:13).

Jesus' friends left him when he needed them most (Matthew 26:56). 'Strike the shepherd, and the sheep will be scattered ...' (Zechariah 13:7).

57

The Lord was accused by people who told lies to get him into trouble (Matthew 26:59-60). 'O God, whom I praise, do not remain silent, for wicked and deceitful men have opened their mouths against me; they have spoken against me with lying tongues' (Psalm 109:1-2).

58

Jesus was struck on the face by his accusers (Matthew 26:67). 'They will strike Israel's ruler on the cheek with a rod' (Micah 5:1).

59

For our sakes, the Lord was beaten and spat on (Luke 22:63, Matthew 26:67). 'I offered my back to those who beat me, my cheeks to those who pulled out my beard; I did not hide my face from mocking and spitting' (Isaiah 50:6).

ZACH'S CHALLENGE

Write out each of these verses then beside each verse write if it is a prophecy about Jesus' birth, life or death. Isaiah 50:6; Isaiah 53:7; Isaiah 53:12; Isaiah 53:9; Isaiah 40:1-5,9; Zechariah 9:9; Isaiah 9:6-7; Isaiah 53:1-3; Zechariah 12:10; Isaiah 7:14; Psalm 41:9; Micah 5:1-2; Genesis 49:10; Zechariah 11:12-13; Isaiah 53:4-6; Jeremiah 23:5.

CHLOE'S QUIZ

On a separate sheet write out the answers. At the end of this quiz you'll be more than half way through the 100 facts! Well done!

48 A woman had her dead child brought back to life. Was it a son or a daughter?

49 What couldn't the poor woman do at all?

50 Who came to the royal official with news that his son had recovered?

51 Who were angry when Jesus healed the blind man?

52 News came to Jesus that his friend Lazarus was what?

53 What relationship did Jesus have with the one who betrayed him?

54 Fill in the missing word. 'So they paid me thirty pieces of _ _ _ _ _ _.'

55 Where did the money go in the end?

56 The Bible talks about the sheep being

s_ _ _ _ _ _ _ _ _ when the shepherd is s _ _ _ _ _ .

57 What did wicked and deceitful men say about Jesus?

They a _ _ _ _ _ _ _ _ him .

58 Where did Jesus' accusers strike him wth a rod?

59 Jesus fulfilled a prophecy in Isaiah that said he would not hide his face from mocking and what else?

Jesus was silent in the presence of those who accused him (Matthew 27:12-14). 'He was oppressed and afflicted, yet he did not open his mouth; he was led like a lamb to the slaughter, and as a sheep before her shearers is silent, so he did not open his mouth' (Isaiah 53:7).

61

His hands and feet were pierced as he was nailed to the cross (Luke 23:33). 'Dogs have surrounded me; a band of evil men has encircled me, they have pierced my hands and my feet' (Psalm 22:16).

62

The Lord Jesus, who had done no wrong, was crucified with wicked men (Mark 15:27). '... he poured out his life unto death, and was numbered with the transgressors' (Isaiah 53:12).

63

People standing round about the crucifixion said that if Jesus trusted in God, he should ask him to save him from the cross (Matthew 27:41-43). 'All who see me mock me; they hurl insults, shaking their heads: "He trusts in the Lord; let the Lord rescue him. Let him deliver him, since he delights in him"' (Psalm 22:7-8).

64

Even on the cross the Lord Jesus prayed for those who were hurting him (Luke 23:34). 'For he bore the sin of many, and made intercession for the transgressors' (Isaiah 53:12).

65

Those who were standing around just shook their heads at him (Matthew 27:39). 'I am an object of scorn to my accusers; when they see me, they shake their heads' (Psalm 109:25).

Jesus' clothes were divided between the solders by them casting lots (John 19:24). 'They divide my garments among them and cast lots for my clothing' (Psalm 22:18).

67

The Lord Jesus was forsaken by his Father as he bore our sins on the cross (Matthew 27:46). 'My God, my God, why have you forsaken me? Why are you so far from saving me, so far from the words of my groaning?' (Psalm 22:1).

It was prophesied that Jesus would be thirsty as he hung there (John 19:28). 'I am worn out calling for help; my throat is parched' (Psalm 69:3).

And hundreds of years before the crucifixion, the psalmist knew that the Lord would be offered gall and vinegar to drink (Matthew 27:34). 'They put gall in my food and gave me vinegar for my thirst' (Psalm 69:21).

70

Jesus' friends were to stand at a distance from the cross (Luke 23:49). 'My friends and companions avoid me because of my wounds; my neighbours stay far away' (Psalm 38:11).

71

Jesus' side was to be pierced (John 19:34). 'But he was pierced for our transgressions, he was crushed for our iniquities; the punishment that brought us peace was upon him, and by his wounds we are healed' (Isaiah 53:5).

CHLOE'S QUIZ

On a separate sheet of paper answer these quiz questions and then complete the challenge.

60 Jesus was led like a lamb to the

_ _ _ _ _ _ _ _ _ _ .

61 A band of evil what surrounded Jesus when he was on the cross?

62 Although Jesus had done no wrong, he was crucified with what kind of men?

63 People stood around what terrible event?

64 What did Jesus do even on the cross?

65 What did the people standing around do with their heads?

66 What was divided between the soldiers?

67 Jesus was _ _ _ _ _ _ _ _ by his father as he bore our sins on the cross.

68 What was it prophesied that Jesus would be as he hung on the cross?

69 What, along with gall, was the Lord offered to drink before he died?

70 Who avoided the Lord as he was being crucified? (three words)

71 What happened to Jesus' side?

ZACH'S CHALLENGE

Draw a grid eighteen spaces wide and ten spaces deep. Fit the answers into the grid to create a word-search. Then find a friend to solve it!

Daylight was to turn to darkness when the Lord was on the cross (Matthew 27:45). "'In that day," declares the Sovereign Lord, "I will make the sun go down at noon and darken the earth in broad daylight"' (Amos 8:9).

And perhaps the most amazing fact of all about the crucifixion of the Lord Jesus Christ is that he died on the cross to save his people from their sins (1 Peter 3:18).

CREATURES GREAT AND SMALL

There are lots of different animals in our world - created by our all-powerful magnificent God. In Psalm 8 the Bible tells us that God has put mankind in charge of creation - 'all flocks and herds, and the beasts of the field, the birds of the air and the fish of the sea.'

74

Think of all the animals you can – from tall giraffes to tiny mice, from huge elephants to slimline snakes, from monkeys with one pair of legs to centipedes, from dogs that bark to bulls that bellow … and the first of all their kinds was made in just ONE day by the Lord our God!

75

All creatures on the earth, mankind included, were made on Day Six of creation. (Genesis 1:24-27)

76

After God made Adam, the Lord brought all the creatures he had made to him to be named. Naming the animals and birds was one of the first jobs the very first man had to do. What a lot of names he had to think up! (Genesis 2:19-20)

77

Did you know that an animal was used by Satan to tempt Eve? In the form of a serpent he persuaded Eve to eat from the tree that God had told Adam and Eve not to eat from. Part of God's curse and punishment of the serpent was 'You will crawl on your belly ... all the days of your life.' So if the serpent only started crawling on his belly after he was cursed, he must have had legs before that! (Genesis 3:14)

When Noah completed the ark according to the building instructions God had given him, the Lord told him to take seven of every clean animal and two of every unclean animal into the ark, as well as seven of every kind of bird. He had to take males and females (of course!) in order that after the flood God's creatures would be able to breed and restock the earth once again. All the animals that live on the earth today are descended from those Noah took into the ark with him. (Genesis 7:2-3)

79

People will argue over anything! But God can use an argument to teach us a lesson. Abraham and his nephew, Lot, were very wealthy men, with a huge amount of livestock between them. There were so many animals that Abraham's herdsmen and Lot's herdsmen began to argue and fight because there wasn't enough grass for all their animals. Abraham, who was a wise man, discussed the problem with his nephew and they decided to separate and live in different parts of the land rather than have their workmen fighting. And the fascinating fact God teaches us from that is that it's better to solve a problem than to fight over it! (Genesis 13:1-11)

God can use animals in answer to prayer. When Abraham was old he wanted to find a good wife for his son, Isaac. Abraham asked his trusted servant to go on a very long journey back to his homeland to find a suitable girl. The servant, who trusted in the Lord, prayed a really strange prayer as he approached a spring of water. He prayed that the right girl would give him a drink of water from the spring and offer to water his camels too. She did, and her name was Rebekah. Rebekah went back home with Abraham's servant and married Isaac. (Genesis 24:12-14)

Pharaoh would not set the Israelite slaves free. He was hard-hearted and God hardened his heart even more. The Lord sent a plague on Egypt every time Pharaoh refused to let God's people go. The second plague was a plague of frogs. They were everywhere! There were frogs in streets and in houses, in beds and in ovens. Frogs even managed to jump into the dishes where bread dough was being mixed! Pharaoh didn't like the frogs one little bit and he told Moses to pray the frogs away and then he would let the people go. Moses prayed and the Lord took away the frogs but Pharaoh did not let the Israelite people go. (Exodus 8:1-15)

The plagues sent by the Lord seemed to harden Pharaoh's heart even more. But each plague brought with it a very special miracle. The Hebrew slaves, God's chosen people, were not affected by the plagues. When one plague killed all the Egyptian livestock the animals that belonged to the Israelites were absolutely fine! (Exodus 9:1-7)

83

Each plague was worse than the one that had gone before, and there were ten altogether. The tenth plague was truly awful. God said that if Pharaoh didn't let the Israelite people go, the oldest child in every Egyptian family, both human and animal, would die. But God had a very different plan for his own special people. He gave instructions for each family to kill a lamb, and to mark round the outside of their house doors with the lamb's blood, before roasting it for a very important feast. The feast was called the Passover, because that night the Lord went throughout Egypt killing the firstborn of every Egyptian family and passing over (that's where the word Passover comes from) each house with lamb's blood around the outside of the door. After that terrible night Pharaoh did let God's people go. (Exodus 12:1-30)

84

Everyone - man, woman, boy and girl, is a sinner and all deserve to be punished by being banished from the Lord our God for time and for eternity. That's a terrible thing. But the Bible tells us an amazing fact. Jesus becomes the Passover Lamb for each and every person who confesses his or her sins and trusts in the Lord as Saviour! And because Jesus is the Christian's Passover Lamb, the believer's punishment is passed over and he goes straight to heaven when he dies and remains there in the joy and glory of Jesus for ever and ever and ever. (1 Corinthians 5:7)

Until Jesus was born, those who wanted to ask God to forgive their sins did so by offering an animal sacrifice. Before they sacrificed the animal, they laid their hand on its head as though passing their sin on to the animal. God told his people to offer animal sacrifices as a picture of what was to come when, on the cross, the Lord Jesus took on himself the sins of all who will believe on him. It is only through his death on the cross that his people's sins are taken away for ever. (Leviticus 1) Some people who lived at the time of the prophet Malachi (400 years before Jesus was born) offered sacrificial animals that were crippled or diseased. They thought that God wouldn't notice! God called those people cheats, and that's exactly what they were. (Malachi 1:8-14)

The Children of Israel were being particularly rebellious. In order to teach them a lesson, God sent poisonous snakes among them. The people realized the snakes had been sent as a punishment and were sorry for what they had said and done. Moses prayed for them and God told him to make a bronze snake and put it on a pole. Anyone who looked on the snake would not die from the effects of venom. Moses did what he was told and made a bronze snake which he attached to a pole. After that, anyone who was bitten by a snake looked at the bronze snake and lived. (Numbers 21:4-9)

CHLOE'S QUIZ

Answer these questions on
a separate sheet of paper.

72 What happened to the
daylight when Jesus was on the cross?

73 On what did Jesus die?

74 How many days did it take God to make
the animals?

75 On which day were animals and mankind
made?

76 One of Adam's first jobs was to name
what?

77. What was the name of the tree Adam was
told not to eat from?

78. How many of every clean animal were to
be taken on to the ark?

79 Whose nephew was Lot?

80 What did Abraham want to find for his son, Isaac?

81 Who would not set the Israelite slaves free?

82. What happened to Pharaoh's heart when the plagues came?

83 Where did the Israelites put the lamb's blood?

84 Jesus is our _ _ _ _ _ _ _ _ Lamb.

85 What kind of sacrifice did God's people offer before Christ's death on the cross?

86 What happened to those who were bitten by venomous snakes and then looked at the bronze snake?

Did you know that a talking donkey once saw an angel? It's a fact! Once a man called Balaam was travelling to a place God didn't want him to go. God sent an angel to stop him. His donkey saw the angel and turned off the road. Balaam was cross and beat her. Then, as they went along a narrow road with walls on both sides, the angel appeared again. The donkey crushed Balaam's foot against the wall as her rider tried to make her go past the angel. Balaam beat her once again. Next the angel stood in the narrowest bit of the road and Balaam's donkey could not get past. She lay down in front of the angel – and was beaten once again. The donkey turned round and asked her master why she had been beaten three times! What a shock Balaam must have had. But it was only when God opened Balaam's eyes to see the angel for himself that he understood why the donkey had behaved as she had. (Numbers 22:21-41)

Samson was one of God's mighty judges. When he was on his way to be married he passed a dead lion. Now, he had been told by the Lord never to touch dead animals, but he went to look at the lion and discovered a swarm of bees in the carcass. He ate some of the honey. Not only did he touch a dead animal, but he ate something from inside it! At the wedding Samson made up a riddle for the young men who were there: 'Out of the eater, something to eat; out of the strong, something sweet.' The young men couldn't answer the riddle – but you can. Out of the eater (the lion that eats other creatures) something to eat (honey); out of the strong (the lion is a very strong animal), something sweet (that honey again). Perhaps you didn't know that there was a riddle in the Bible. (Judges 14:8-20)

David was still a young man when he killed Goliath, but that was not the first brave thing he had done. 'When a lion or a bear came and carried off a sheep from the flock, I went after it, struck it and rescued the sheep from its mouth. When it turned on me, I seized it by its hair, struck it and killed both the lion and the bear.' David knew where his power came from, 'The Lord who delivered me from the paw of the lion and the paw of the bear will deliver me from the hand of this Philistine (Goliath).'
And he did!
(1 Samuel 17:34-37)

The Book of Job in the Bible is the story of a man to whom terrible things happened. Poor Job was in a bad way, made even worse by his three friends who came to help and comfort him. Unfortunately they knew exactly the wrong things to say and were no comfort at all. Eventually God spoke directly to Job, reminding him that it is the Lord who provides food for the ravens, who watches the deer as her fawn is born, who makes the great wings of the ostrich, who gives the horse its strength and the grasshopper its ability to leap so high. Because of all his problems Job was looking in at himself rather than God. By pointing his servant to the wonders of his creation, the Lord pointed him back to himself. When you feel that life is getting on top of you, look around at God's wonderful world and remember that the One who made it is more wonderful still. (Job 39)

The Kingdom of God is so amazing that we can only imagine it in pictures. One picture God gives of his kingdom is of wolves and lambs, cows and bears living happily together, of lions eating straw rather than killing prey, and of little children playing safely right beside a cobra's hole. (Isaiah 11:6-8)

Through the prophet Ezekiel, God warned bad shepherds who looked after their sheep so poorly that the creatures scattered and were lost. The bad shepherds were the leaders of God's people, and they weren't leading them in the right way. God told Ezekiel that he would rescue the sheep himself. And he did – when Jesus came to be our Good Shepherd. (Ezekiel 34:1-24)

93

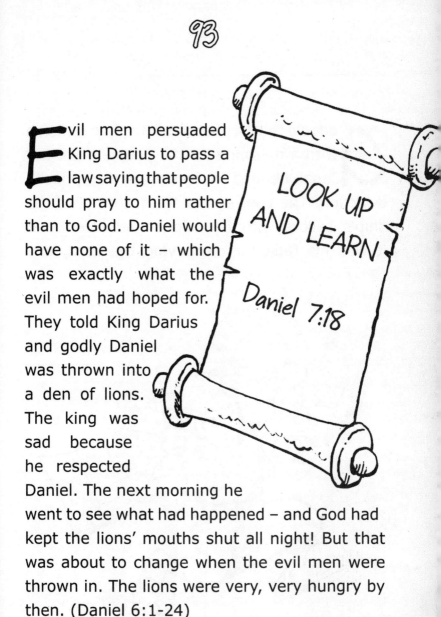

LOOK UP AND LEARN

Daniel 7:18

Evil men persuaded King Darius to pass a law saying that people should pray to him rather than to God. Daniel would have none of it – which was exactly what the evil men had hoped for. They told King Darius and godly Daniel was thrown into a den of lions. The king was sad because he respected Daniel. The next morning he went to see what had happened – and God had kept the lions' mouths shut all night! But that was about to change when the evil men were thrown in. The lions were very, very hungry by then. (Daniel 6:1-24)

94

God told the Prophet Jonah to go to Nineveh with a message for the people there but Jonah headed off, by ship, in the opposite direction. The Lord sent a storm that filled the ship's sailors with fear. Jonah admitted that it was his fault for disobeying the Lord, and

agreed to be thrown overboard into the sea. A big fish was sent to save Jonah's life. The fish swallowed Jonah before vomiting him up on dry land near Nineveh. It would have been so much easier if Jonah had done what the Lord wanted him to do first time round! (Jonah 1:15-2:10)

Jesus told a story one day in order to teach a fascinating fact. He said that when the Son of Man (that's the Lord himself) comes back in glory there will be a great day of judgement in which people will be divided into two groups, just as a shepherd separates his sheep from his goats. The sheep will be taken into heaven and the goats will be sent to hell. The sheep are God's people who trust in him and live their lives for him. The goats are those who have not trusted and believed in the Lord Jesus. (Matthew 25:31-46)

One day the Lord told a story about his love. In the story he was a shepherd who searched the countryside until he found his sheep that had wandered away and got lost. Jesus is our Good Shepherd and he died on the cross in order that his lost sheep could be taken home to heaven one day. And that's amazing love! (Luke 15:1-7)

Someone has said that donkeys really are beasts of burden – but sometimes they are awkward beasts and don't like carrying their loads. Despite that, Jesus used a young donkey that had never been ridden before to ride into Jerusalem. The donkey however didn't object and did what its Maker wanted it to do. (John 12:14-15)

When the Apostle John was an old man, God gave him a vision of heaven. In the vision John saw a living lamb, that had been killed and brought to life again, being worshipped. Jesus is the Lamb of God, the Passover Lamb through whom alone anyone can go to heaven. And when Christian people reach their heavenly home they will worship Jesus, the Lamb of God. (Revelation 5:8-14)

TWO PROMISES

99

Remember God's promises are facts - because what God promises will happen!

Let the wicked forsake his way and the evil man his thoughts. Let him turn to the Lord, and he will have mercy on him, and to our God, for he will freely pardon (Isaiah 55:7).

100

If anyone does sin, we have one who speaks to the Father in our defence – Jesus Christ, the Righteous One (1 John 2:1).

CHLOE'S QUIZ

87 On what kind of animal was Balaam travelling?

88 Inside what did Samson discover bees nesting?

89 David killed a lion and a __ __ __ __ when he was keeping his father's sheep safe.

90 What creature is strong?

91 A lovely picture of God's kingdom is of wolves and lambs, cows and what living happily together?

92 God warned against shepherds who looked after what poorly?

93 What creatures had their mouths kept shut all night by God?

94 Inside what creature was Jonah kept safe for three days?

95 God will divide all people into two groups. Those who believe in him are called sheep – what is the other group made up of?

96 Jesus told a story about a good shepherd who went searching for what?

97 What are beasts of burden?

98 What animal is used as a picture of Jesus?

99 Who should wicked and evil people turn to?

100 Who is the Righteous One?

Answers

1 Biblia

2 Berith

3 Genesis

4 Abraham

5 Isaac

6 Jacob

7 House of God

8 Israel

9 Exodus

10 River Nile

11 I am that I am

12 Manna

13 Levites

14 Numbers

15 Deuteros

16 Joshua

17 Samuel

18 Chronicle

19 Babylon

20 Jerusalem

21 Courage

22 Wisdom

23 Prophets

24 Jeremiah

25 Luke

26 Apostles

27 Paul

28 Philemon

29 Hebrews

30 Jesus

31 Heaven

32 Bethlehem

33 Immanuel

34 Myrrh

35 Egypt

36 Rachel

37 A miracle

38 Leprosy

39 Healed her

40 Demons

41 Furious

42 Twelve

43 Amazed

44 In the tombs

45 Leftover food

46 Hearing and speech

47 Blind

48 Son

49 Straighten up

50 Servants

51 The teachers of the law

52 Sick

53 Friend

54 Silver

55 To the potter

56 Scattered; Struck

57 Accused

58 On the cheek

59 Spitting

60 Slaughter

61 Men

62 Thieves or Wicked men

63 The Crucifixion

64 He prayed

65 Shook their heads

66 Clothes

67 Forsaken

68 Thirsty

69 Vinegar

70 Friends, Companions and Neighbours

71 It was pierced

72 It turned to darkness

73 The cross

74 One

75 Day six

76 The animals

77. The tree of the knowledge of Good and Evil

78. Seven

79 Abraham's

80 A wife

81 Pharaoh

82 It got harder and harder

83 On the outside of their house doors

84 Passover

85 Animal sacrifice

86 They lived

87 Donkey

88 A lion

89 Bear

90 Horse

91 Lion

92 Their sheep

93 Lions

94 A big fish (or whale)

95 Goats

96 A lost sheep

97 Donkeys

98 A lamb

99 God the Father

100 Jesus Christ

ABBI'S EXTRA BITS
The Names of Jesus

We all have different names at different times. When we are babies our parents often use pet names for us. When we fall in love we might find ourselves called Sweetheart or Darling, and perhaps one day Dad or Mum and even Grandfather or Grandmother. For very different reasons the Lord Jesus has many names. They make a fascinating study. Let's take a look at some of them...

Remember Job and all his troubles? Even when he was in this terrible situation, he made a wonderful statement about Jesus, who would not be born for hundreds of years to come. He said, 'I know that my Redeemer lives, and that in the end he will stand upon the earth. And after my skin has been destroyed, yet in my flesh I will see God; I myself will see him with my own eyes – I, and not another. How my heart yearns within me!' (Job 19:25-27)

A redeemer is someone who buys something. The Lord showed Job that his soul would be bought by Jesus and that one day he would see his Redeemer face to face.

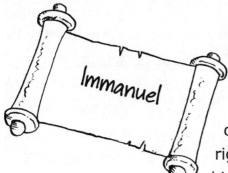

It's amazing but true that God gave his people information about the coming of the Lord Jesus right throughout history. It was between 700 and 800 years before Jesus was born at Bethlehem that Isaiah talked of him coming and said he would be called 'Immanuel' (Isaiah 7:14). And when Jesus was born on earth that's just what he was, God in human flesh living among ordinary human beings! Immanuel means God with us.

Another name for Jesus is 'Wonderful Counsellor.' We all know what wonderful means and a counsellor is someone who advises and leads. Is Jesus your Wonderful Counsellor? Do you take his advice and follow him? (Isaiah 9:6)

Isaiah called Jesus 'Mighty God.' Do you know that there are some people who think that Jesus was just a good man! They can't possibly have read the Bible or they would know that he did things that only God can do. Even the very best of men can't feed more than 5,000 hungry people from a handful of bread rolls and a couple of small fish! (Isaiah 9:6)

Strangely Isaiah then called Jesus 'Everlasting Father.' How can Jesus be God the Father as well as being God's Son? Isaiah had no way of really understanding it, but this is one of the Old Testament clues that help us to understand that, while God is one God, he is three persons – the Father, the Son and the Holy Spirit. (Isaiah 9:6)

Isaiah also calls the Lord Jesus 'Prince of Peace.' That's a great name for Jesus whose death on the cross brings peace of heart to those who come to him for forgiveness, and gives them peace with God because he washes away all their sins. (Isaiah 9:6)

Isaiah also told the people a rather puzzling name for Jesus, their deliverer. Isaiah referred to him as 'a man of sorrows.' If you think about what the Lord Jesus did for us on the cross, you'll realise some of the sorrows he suffered for us. (Isaiah 53:3)

Another Old Testament prophet called Zechariah called Jesus a fountain that would cleanse his people from sin and impurity. What does 'a fountain' do? The water in a fountain can be used for washing. When we come to the Lord Jesus in faith he washes us from all our dirty sins, and all our sins look filthy to God. (Zechariah 13:1)

Four hundred years before Jesus' birth, Malachi called Jesus 'the sun of righteousness' and said he would rise with healing in his wings. The sun that shines in the sky helps keep us healthy. Jesus heals his people from their terrible sin-sickness by forgiving them fully and for ever. (Malachi 4:2)

Son of God

What a surprise it must have been to Mary to be told by an angel that she was to have a baby even though she was young and not married. This baby would be made by the power of God. He would not have a human father. Mary's child would be called 'the Son of God'! (Luke 1:35)

Jesus Saviour

Months before the Lord was born at Bethlehem, an angel spoke to Joseph and told him that Mary was to have a special baby, the Son of God, and that his name was to be Jesus. Mary and Joseph didn't choose the baby's name, God told them what to call him. Why? Because in the Hebrew language the name Jesus means Saviour, and the angel told Joseph that the baby would save his people from their sins. (Matthew 1:21)

The Word

When John began his gospel he didn't start with the birth of Jesus. He opened the story of the life of Jesus with the words, 'In the beginning was the Word, and the Word was with God, and the Word was God.' Right back at the beginning of the Bible God created by his Word. Who was that Word? He was Jesus. He was right in there at creation all those years before he was born at Bethlehem. Some things are almost too wonderful to take in! (John 1:1)

The Lamb

John the Baptist baptised Jesus in the River Jordan. His special name for him was 'the Lamb of God.' Do you remember the story of the Passover lamb? Jesus is our Passover Lamb. Because his blood was shed on the cross all those who put their trust in him will live forever and ever in heaven. He is indeed the Lamb of God. (John 1:29)

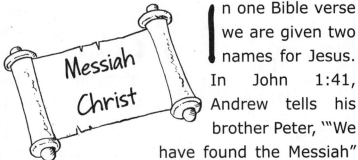

In one Bible verse we are given two names for Jesus. In John 1:41, Andrew tells his brother Peter, '"We have found the Messiah" (that is the Christ).' The Jews knew that God had promised a Saviour would come. They referred to him as the Messiah, which means the one specially appointed by God to be the great deliverer of his people. The name Christ means just the same thing in Greek.

One day two blind men called out to Jesus to help them. They shouted, 'Have mercy on us, Son of David.' They knew God had promised that a special son from the family of King David would come to save his people. They recognised Jesus was that one. Isn't it interesting that two blind men could see in their hearts and minds what sighted people could not see? (Matthew 9:27)

135

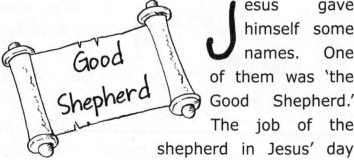

Jesus gave himself some names. One of them was 'the Good Shepherd.' The job of the shepherd in Jesus' day was to care for the sheep regardless of his own health and safety. Jesus went on to say, 'The good shepherd lays down his life for the sheep.' That's exactly what he did. Nobody took the Lord's life from him, he laid down his own life in order to take the punishment for the sins of his people so that they could go free and go to heaven. What a Good Shepherd Jesus is! (John 10:11)

This is a name that Jesus called himself. We all need food to live on earth, but if we want to live in heaven we need food that will keep us alive for ever. Jesus is that food. Reading God's Word should be as important to us as eating our dinner! (John 6:35)

The True Vine

Another of Jesus' unusual names for himself is 'the true vine'. He says that those who believe in him are the branches! Are you a branch in Jesus? What does he mean by that? The Lord is telling us that if we want to be fruitful in our lives we need to be attached to him. We are attached to Jesus when we trust him as our Saviour. Not only does Jesus say that he is the true vine and we are the branches, he tells us that his father is the gardener! So God the Father is like a gardener looking after all those who are attached to Jesus. (John 15:1-4) If you read Galatians 5:22-23, you'll discover the kind of fruit that our heavenly Gardener will produce in our lives.

The Apostle Paul wrote of Jesus as 'the Rock.' Jesus told a story which says that houses built on rocks never sink into the ground whereas houses built on sand are washed away in the first flood. Lives built on the rock that is Jesus are safe for all eternity. Lives built on any other foundation will eventually come to grief (1 Corinthians 10:4).

Another name for Jesus is the 'Mediator.' What does that mean? A mediator is a go-between, someone who sorts out things between two people. None of us can approach God because we are such awful sinners. Jesus is our go-between, or Mediator, through whom we can come to God because he has taken away the sins of his people that are such an offence to God (1 Timothy 2:5).

The last book of the Bible is a vision John was given of heaven. In it Jesus gives us a strange name for himself. He says he is 'the Alpha and the Omega.' If you knew Greek it would not be so strange. Alpha and omega are the first and the last letters of the Greek alphabet just like our A and Z. Jesus is using this name for himself to show that he is eternal, that he was there before the beginning of things and that he will be there forever (Revelation 1:8).

And here's a fact – there are many other names in the Bible for Jesus. You'll find some of them in Matthew 2:23, 8:20, John 8:12, 10:7, 14:6 and Hebrews 12:2.

Author Information

Irene Howat is an accomplished writer for children and adults. She has many titles to her name. She is married to a minister and they have a grown-up family. She is also a talented artist who lives in Ayrshire, Scotland. She especially enjoys getting letters from children and replies to all of them!

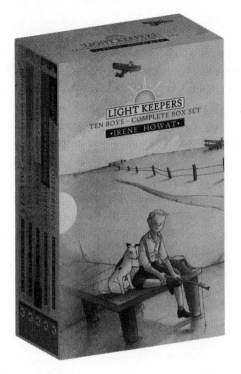

Lightkeeper's Box Set for Boys
ISBN: 978-1-84550-318-5

Five books by Irene Howat in a gift box presentation set. A great present for Christmas or birthday includes: Ten Boys who Changed the World; Ten Boys who Didn't Give In; Ten Boys who Made a Difference; Ten Boys who Made History; Ten Boys who Used Their Talents. Each book has 10 short biographies of inspirational lives which will serve as an example – books include fact files, prayer suggestions and quizzes.

Lightkeeper's Box Set for Girls
ISBN: 978-1-84550-319-2

Five books by Irene Howat in a gift box presentation set. A great present for Christmas or birthday includes: Ten Girls who Changed the World; Ten Girls who Didn't Give In; Ten Girls who Made a Difference; Ten Girls who Made History; Ten Girls who Used Their Talents. Each book has 10 short biographies of inspirational lives which will serve as an example – books include fact files, prayer suggestions and quizzes.

The Singing Soldiers
ISBN: 978-1-84550-249-2

You wouldn't send a choir into a battle. Would you set up a sing-song in a stinking old jail? Singing would be the last thing on your mind! Well, real people in the Bible did exactly that and some modern day children find out all about them. The Singing Soldiers retells the story of Jehoshaphat; Paul and Silas; Moses and the Red Sea; David and King Saul and Job.

CHRISTIAN FOCUS PUBLICATIONS

Christian Focus | Christian Heritage | CF4K | Mentor

Christian Focus Publications publishes books for adults and children under its four main imprints: Christian Focus, Christian Heritage, CF4K and Mentor. Our books reflect that God's word is reliable and Jesus is the way to know him, and live for ever with him.

Our children's publication list includes a Sunday school curriculum that covers pre-school to early teens; puzzle and activity books. We also publish personal and family devotional titles, biographies and inspirational stories that children will love.

If you are looking for quality Bible teaching for children then we have an excellent range of Bible story and age specific theological books. From pre-school to teenage fiction, we have it covered!

**Find us at our web page:
www.christianfocus.com**

CF4•K
*Because you're never
too young to know Jesus*